# HOLY
# ISLAND

M. Scott Weightman

> Bless O Lord this island,
> This Holy Island.
> Make it a place of peace
> and love.
> Make it a place of joy and
> light.
> Make it a place of holiness
> and hospitality.
> Make it a place of grace
> and goodness
> And begin with me. ☩

After years of exile in Scotland Oswald, King of Northumbria, defeated Cadwallon, King of North Wales, in AD634. He thus reunited his kingdom and established Northumbrian supremacy from the Humber to the Forth.

As a Christian convert, Oswald wished to evangelize his people and sent to Iona for a missionary. Abbot Segenius first sent Corman, an austere monk who, finding the Northumbrians barbarous and obstinate, soon returned to Scotland. So in 635 Aidan, an Irish monk, volunteered to replace him. He chose Lindisfarne as the site for his church and monastery; it was close to the capital, Bebbanburgh (today's Bamburgh) and secure in its island position. From here he preached the gospel throughout Northumbria, with King Oswald sometimes acting as his interpreter.

The mission flourished. People gave lands for churches and monasteries to be founded. Children were often sent to Lindisfarne to be educated by the Scottish monks. Four brothers who arrived there, Cynebil, Caelin, Cedd and Chad, became priests, the last two of these being made bishops. Cedd founded churches and monasteries in Essex and north Yorkshire.

Chad was sent to Ireland by Aidan and, having completed his studies, returned to Northumbria. He was a devout and gentle man, similar to Aidan in his devotion to work. After his death in 672, he was venerated as a saint. Pilgrims visited his tomb in the belief that it held powers of healing.

Aidan's mission on Lindisfarne changed the Northumbrian people. According to the chronicler Bede, many Northumbrians, both noble and simple, laid aside their weapons, preferring to follow the way of the cross rather than study the art of war. Missionaries trained by Aidan travelled throughout Britain, some even journeying to the Netherlands.

*RIGHT: A Celtic cross frames the head of St Aidan. In one hand he holds a torch, symbolizing the light of the Gospel, in the other his bishop's crozier.*

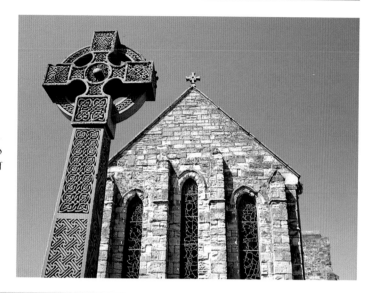

RIGHT: St Mary's parish church. The vicar, Canon David Adam, wrote a prayer of St Aidan, opposite. His book Fire of the North is an illustrated biography of St Cuthbert.

During Aidan's lifetime, communities of nuns were founded in Northumbria. Hild, the first Northumbrian woman to take the veil, was appointed Abbess of Hartlepool.

After Aidan there was a bishop at Lindisfarne for almost 250 years. During this time nine saints and 16 bishops were associated with Lindisfarne. The sixth bishop, Cuthbert, was to earn the greatest fame ✠

Bamburgh Castle. Bede records that, while meditating on the Inner Farne in 642, Aidan saw the Mercian army led by Penda attacking Bamburgh Castle. St Aidan prayed and the wind changed to blow the flames in the faces of the pagans.

On the night St Aidan died in 651, Cuthbert was tending sheep in the Lammermuir hills. According to the Venerable Bede 'he saw a stream of light from the sky . . . in the midst of this the choir of the heavenly host descended to the earth, and taking with them, without delay, a soul of exceeding brightness.'

When Cuthbert learned that Aidan had died at the very time of his vision, he immediately left his flock to join the monastery at nearby Melrose, the first and most famous of Aidan's foundations.

After a brief time at Ripon, Cuthbert returned to Melrose Abbey where he and the prior, Boisil, caught the yellow plague. Boisil died, but Cuthbert was spared to continue his remarkable ministry.

For nine years from 676 Cuthbert followed Aidan's example and sought seclusion on Inner Farne, in a cell and oratory designed to isolate him from anything which might distract him from his prayers and meditation. During this time he is said to have performed miracles through the strength of his prayer, many of them recorded by Bede.

**ABOVE:** *King Ecgfrith visited Cuthbert on the Inner Farne to persuade him to accept the bishopric of Hexham. Cuthbert refused, but a compromise was reached. Eata, Bishop of Lindisfarne, became Bishop of Hexham and Cuthbert was appointed to the vacant see of Lindisfarne.*

Cuthbert's love for all animals and birds is legendary. His name is particularly associated with the eider duck (Cuddy's) and the otter. Once, Cuthbert was discovered having walked into the sea up to his armpits to spend the night praying and singing hymns. According to Bede, the following morning two otters dried his feet and warmed his frozen legs.

In 685 Cuthbert was eventually persuaded to become Bishop of Lindisfarne. After his enthronement at York, he strove to bring a new unity to the Church in Northumbria, but in 687 returned to the solitude of Inner Farne, where eventually he died. His body was buried by the altar in Lindisfarne's priory.

The first Viking raid on England was directed at Holy Island in 793. Symeon of Durham records 'They came like stinging hornets, like ravening wolves, they made raids on all sides, slaying not only cattle but priests and

**BELOW:** *A re-enactment in the priory grounds of the Viking invasion of 793.*

monks. They came to the church at Lindisfarne and laid all waste, trampled the Holy places with polluted feet, dug down the altars and bore away the treasures of the church. Some of the brethren they slew, some they carried away captive, some they drove out naked after mocking and vexing them. Some they drowned in the sea.' The survivors rebuilt the church but Northumbria gradually lost its power and influence. In 875 the monks fled the monastery for fear of further invasion, in their terror taking with them their precious holy relics: the body of St Cuthbert, the skull of King Oswald, some of St Aidan's bones and the Lindisfarne Gospels. It is probable that the island's laymen also fled to the mainland.

During the next 300 years, St Cuthbert's body was several times moved by the monks to protect it from the ravages of invaders. In 1070 it was taken to Durham and has been there ever since. Over the centuries, the body has been disturbed on several occasions to satisfy curiosity about its remarkable preservation. In 1537 it was reported to be 'sound, sweet, odoriferous and flexible', 840 years after Cuthbert's death ☩

BELOW: *The final resting place of St Cuthbert in Durham Cathedral.*

ABOVE: *A window in Durham Cathedral illustrating St Cuthbert's love for wild life.*

MAIN PICTURE: *St Cuthbert's Isle can be reached at low tide. Bede says that Cuthbert used a small chapel here. Today the site of its altar is marked by a wooden cross.*

SAINT CUTHBERT · BISHOP OF LINDISFARNE

The 6th and 7th centuries were a period of outstanding brilliance for Northumbrian arts. The priory museum contains much from this 'golden age' including sculptured stone crosses and intricate figure carvings with vine-scroll ornamentation interwined with birds and beasts.

However, without doubt the crowning achievement of the ancient Northumbrians was the magnificently illuminated manuscripts known as the Lindisfarne Gospels, one of the finest surviving examples of Celtic art. They were written in honour of St Cuthbert by Eadfrith, Bishop of Lindisfarne 698–721.

*BELOW: In his little scriptorium at the monastery on Lindisfarne the master scribe, Eadfrith, had only the most basic materials with which to write the Lindisfarne Gospels.*

*ABOVE: A page at the beginning of St Matthew's Gospel. It is incomplete, the 'er' of the first line being only partially painted.*

Around 130 calf-hides were scraped and cured to produce the vellum sheets on which the Gospels were written, mainly in Latin. Pens were made from feathers while the black ink was a combination of soot and egg whites. Plants and mineral pigments provided the colours for the illuminations. The binding was richly adorned with jewels and gold.

When the monks fled from the Danes in 875, they took the Gospels

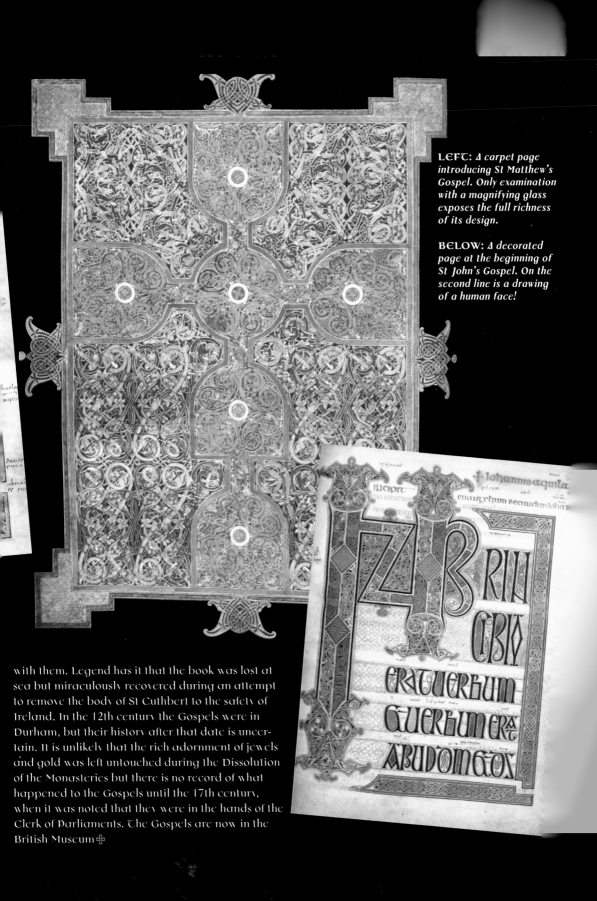

**LEFT:** *A carpet page introducing St Matthew's Gospel. Only examination with a magnifying glass exposes the full richness of its design.*

**BELOW:** *A decorated page at the beginning of St John's Gospel. On the second line is a drawing of a human face!*

with them. Legend has it that the book was lost at sea but miraculously recovered during an attempt to remove the body of St Cuthbert to the safety of Ireland. In the 12th century the Gospels were in Durham, but their history after that date is uncertain. It is unlikely that the rich adornment of jewels and gold was left untouched during the Dissolution of the Monasteries but there is no record of what happened to the Gospels until the 17th century, when it was noted that they were in the hands of the Clerk of Parliaments. The Gospels are now in the British Museum ✠

# The Benedictine Priory

Lindisfarne's Celtic monastery was a simple affair – beehive shaped huts made of wood and wattle. Nearby would have been a small thatched church in an enclosure also containing a refectory, kitchen, dormitory, guest house and writing room.

After the monks fled in 875, the island probably remained uninhabited for over 200 years. In 1082 Benedictine monks were granted the see and renamed Lindisfarne 'Holy Island' to commemorate the holy blood shed during the Viking invasions. By 1120, they had rebuilt the ruined priory, dedicating its church to St Cuthbert. Most of the sandstone used came from Goswick on the mainland. The buildings surrounding the cloister garth were built in the 13th century, those of the outer court in the later Middle Ages. In the 15th century the apse was demolished and a longer oblong chancel built.

Under the Benedictines, Holy Island for 450 years escaped the attacks of marauding Scots. The extensive mainland parish of Lindisfarne fared less well. At the Dissolution in 1537, the Crown assumed control of the island, having closed the priory down. The prior was made Bishop of Berwick. Lindisfarne immediately became used as a stronghold and in 1543 an army was assembled there to repel the Scots. The priory was destroyed to provide stone for a new castle. The church was converted into a storehouse. In 1613 the Earl of Dunbar ransacked what remained of the priory, removing amongst other things the bells and the roof lead. The ship bearing this booty away sank shortly after departure, with much loss of life, the event taken to be an act of God's displeasure.

The roofless ruin of the Norman church is the most spectacular feature of what remains of an elegant and impressive priory. The church was cruciform in shape. At the crossing a magnificent vaulting rib remains, the

**BELOW:** *This splendid 11th-century entrance through the west front of the church is unmistakably Norman in design.*

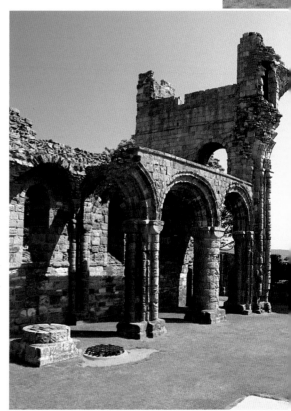

**ABOVE:** *Beyond the Benedictine priory is St Mary's parish church. St Cuthbert's Isle is just offshore while the Cheviot hills are seen in the distance.*

**INSET:** *A 13th-century glazed-ware face found near the priory. It was probably the handle of a drinking vessel.*

**LEFT:** *The north wall of the ruined priory. The Rainbow Arch, set diagonally over the transept, marks the former location of the central tower.*

Rainbow Arch. This and the design on the arch and pillars in the church suggest that it was built by the same monks who built Durham Cathedral. The monks' living quarters were clustered around a cloister on the south side of the church. On the left of the south transept are the remains of a small spiral staircase, the night stairs used by the monks to go to services straight from their dormitory. The design of the monastery is basically Benedictine with local adaptations; for example, the entrance to the cloister from the court on the south side has a gate strengthened by a barbican as a measure against Scottish raiders. To the east of the cloister was the chapter house, on the west were the domestic areas, kitchen, brew house, pantry, cellars, larder and a bakehouse. On the south side was the dining hall and, in the outer court, the guest house ✠

*Sunrise over the castle,
which retained a garrison
until 1820 when it was
adapted for use as a
coastguard station.*

For with the flow and ebb, its style
  varies from continent to isle;
Dry-shod, o'er sands, twice every day,
  the pilgrims to the shrine find way;
Twice every day the waves efface
  of staves and sandall'd feet the trace.

Sir Walter Scott: *Marmion*

**ABOVE:** *The parish church of St Mary stands only 16 metres (50 feet) away from the priory church. Today it is the focal point of the religious life on the island for locals, pilgrims and tourists.*

**RIGHT:** *The chancel. The carpet before the altar reproduces a carpet page of the Lindisfarne Gospels. The reredos depicts figures of many Northern saints.*

The parish church of St Mary was built between 1120 and 1145. Today, original Norman architecture remains in the form of three arches on the eastern side of the north aisle. The chancel is 13th-century and there is a medieval tombstone, decorated with a cross and a sword, on the north wall. A small belfry was added to the church at the beginning of the 18th century.

A Victorian traveller, Dr George Johnston, wrote of the church in 1854: 'The church is cold, damp and musty within: the walls covered with green mould and scalters [insects of some sort] were crawling on the paved floor. The seats are unfitted for the service, so much so that neither male nor female can kneel at any part of it. Every seat has a large brass plate, engraved with the name of its proprietors: and the Border Brewery has three seats to its share.' Soon after Johnston's visit a major restoration was carried out and completed in 1860.

The church has two porches. Until 1886 the north porch, now a vestry, was used as a mortuary for bodies recovered from the sea.

The beautiful carpet before the altar was designed to reproduce a page of the Lindisfarne Gospels. The work was directed by Miss Kathleen Darbury. Students from Alnwick College of Education transferred the design onto canvas and 18 women from the island completed the needlework. The carpet was dedicated in 1970. In the same year Rockford College Community, Illinois, presented a copy of the Lindisfarne Gospels to the people of Holy Island ✠

+In memory of Edward de Stein Knight 1887-1965 and Miss Gladys de Stein 1891-1968 +

LEFT: *A stained-glass window in the west wall of the parish church, depicting St Aidan. It is dedicated to the memory of the de Stein family, who owned the castle until 1944.*

BELOW: *The sandstone used for the priory church was brought from Cheswick on the mainland. Wagons and ox-carts were used. Later monastic buildings shown in the foreground were constructed from the grey limestone of the island.*

# The Castle

The first mention of any castle or fort appears in a border survey of 1550, which mentions the 'Fort of Beblowe' (the ancient name of the hill on which the castle is built). The building was begun during the reign of Henry VIII, using stone from the priory. Robert Rooke of Berwick superintended the first fortifications, which followed an order in council that 'all havens should be fensed with bulwarkes and bloke houses against the Scots'. In 1543 a large army led by Edward Seymour, Earl of Hertford, (brother of Henry VIII's third wife, Jane Seymour) was based at the castle in order to fight the Scots. The expedition formed on the island also included ten line-of-battle ships at anchor in the harbour.

After the union of England and Scotland in 1603, the strategic importance of the castle diminished, although it remained in use as a garrison. In 1639 an officer of the King visited, remarking on the good maintenance of the fort and its armaments. He noted a force of 24 soldiers and that 'the captain at our being there was Captain Rugg, known commonly by his great nose'.

At the beginning of the Civil War the castle was a Royalist stronghold but soon fell to the Parliamentarians. The next recorded incident was a micro-battle of 1715. Having been reduced to a garrison of only seven men, five of

**BELOW:** *Lindisfarne Castle, owned by the National Trust, is a fort perched on the highest point of the island, Beblowe Crag. This outcrop was formed when molten dolerite from nearby Cheviot forced its way through a fracture in the sandstone.*

whom were absent at the time, the castle was captured by two Jacobites, Launcelot Errington and his nephew Mack. Unfortunately the reinforcements they expected failed to arrive and the two men eventually surrendered to a force of soldiers sent from Berwick to retake the stronghold.

By 1820, the castle's use as a fortification was over. The guns were removed and it was partially dismantled. Later it served as a coastguard station, but in the 1880s Edward Hudson, proprietor of *Country Life* magazine, bought the building as a private residence, later restored by Sir Edwin Lutyens in characteristic style. In 1944, the then owners, Sir Edward de Stein and his sister, Gladys, gave the castle to the National Trust. The de Steins are commemorated by a stained-glass window in the parish church of St Mary ✠

ABOVE: *The barrel-vaulted drawing room is now known as the 'Ship' room because of the fine 1840 model of a Dutch vessel,* Henrietta of Amsterdam, *that Sir Edwin Lutyens suspended from the ceiling.*

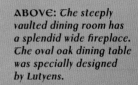

ABOVE: *The steeply vaulted dining room has a splendid wide fireplace. The oval oak dining table was specially designed by Lutyens.*

**ABOVE:** *Every Easter, Christian pilgrims walk across the mud-flats at low tide.*

**BELOW:** *A reconstruction of an open-topped refuge box, used on the Pilgrims Way before the construction of the present causeway.*

The route across the Holy Island sands to Chare Ends, used in the time of Saints Aidan and Cuthbert, remains the only access to the mainland. Tides sweep across the sands with great speed and the parish register records several deaths of unwary travellers caught by the rising waters. The crossing remained virtually unchanged until the beginning of the 20th century, the only improvement having been in 1860 when posts were erected to mark the route across the sands for the benefit of pilgrims, strangers and islanders alike.

While most people walked across in those days, the postmaster and two innkeepers owned pony carts which they hired out. At high tide boats were used. In 1920, the telephone came to Lindisfarne.

With the advent of the motor car the pony and traps were replaced by taxis, specially raised to avoid damage from sea water. In 1954 the causeway was opened, forming a permanent man-made link with the mainland. The road was extended in 1965 and the part crossing the South Low channel was raised above the level of the sands.

Nevertheless, the tide still floods the causeway and can still trap unsuspecting visitors. The box built to provide a refuge from the encroaching water is still used, particularly in the summer months. So, for two hours before high tide and three and a half hours after, the link with the mainland is rendered impassable.

Thus the sea enforces the island community's traditional independence and unique identity. This is most apparent in winter when the crowds have left and the island assumes once again the air of a place at peace apart from the rest of Britain ✠

MAIN PICTURE: *Used by taxis and pony traps until 1954, the Pilgrims Way was the most direct route from the mainland to Chare Ends.*

BELOW LEFT: *Tradition has it that eider ducks were St Cuthbert's favourite birds, known on the island as Cuddy's ducks.*

BELOW CENTRE: *Local horsemen use the mud-flats to exercise their horses, particularly in winter when their usual training areas are frost covered.*

BELOW RIGHT: *Tide tables are provided at both ends of the causeway, in the village and local press. The enclosed white refuge box is still sometimes used by people caught by the tide.*

FAR LEFT: *The Ouse (or harbour). Salmon and shellfish are still caught by island boats but the fishing industry is no longer crucial to the economy of the island.*

LEFT: *In the past, island fisherwomen took fish to sell on the mainland, travelling perhaps for two days until all were sold.*

BOTTOM LEFT: *The Fisherman's Cottage Museum in Front Street relates the life of a 19th-century island fisherman.*

MAIN PICTURE: *Upturned herring boats are now used for storage.*

ABOVE: *When sailors align these two beacons on Old Law, on the mainland, they get a bearing for safe entry into Holy Island harbour.*

BELOW: *It is said the Snook tower must have housed winding-gear for an 18th-century coal mine, but there is no sign of a shaft.*

*Limekilns at Castle Point. As early as 1344 the quarrying of limestone was recorded, and in 1860 the Dundee Company built a new landing-jetty below the castle.*

**ABOVE:** *This 9th-century grave marker shows seven warriors, probably Vikings.*

**RIGHT:** *An aerial view of the southern half of the island.*

**RIGHT (inset):** *The image of King Oswald of Northumbria. The fascinating story of Lindisfarne is told in the English Heritage Priory Museum.*

**ABOVE and RIGHT:** *It is said that mead was originally made by the island's monks. The Lindisfarne Mead Company produces not only mead but also liqueur, honey, lemon curd, marmalade and fudge. Visitors can sample the products in the showroom.*